Hard Work

A Day with Paramedics

By Jan Kottke

Welcome Books

Children's Press
A Division of Grolier Publishing
New York / London / Hong Kong / Sydney
Danbury, Connecticut

Photo Credits: All photos by Thaddeus Harden
Contributing Editor: Jennifer Ceaser
Book Design: Michael DeLisio

Visit Children's Press on the Internet at:
http://publishing.grolier.com

Library of Congress Cataloging-in-Publication Data

Kottke, Jan.
    A day with paramedics / by Jan Kottke.
      p. cm. — (Hard work)
    Includes bibliographical references and index.
    Summary: Explains in simple terms some of the work that paramedics do.
    ISBN 0-516-23091-3 (lib. bdg.) — ISBN 0-516-23016-6 (pbk.)
    1. Emergency medical technicians—Juvenile literature. 2. Emergency medical
services—Juvenile literature. [1. Emergency medical technicians. 2. Occupations.] I.Title.

RA645.5.K68 2000
362.18—dc21

00-024383

Contents

My name is Tony.

This is my partner, Beatrice.

We are **paramedics**.

We help people who are sick or hurt.

We work in an **ambulance**.

We get a call on the radio.

A call means someone needs help.

It's an **emergency**!

Someone is sick.

We drive fast to where the emergency is.

We are here!

We put the emergency **kit** on the **stretcher**.

We pull the stretcher out of the ambulance.

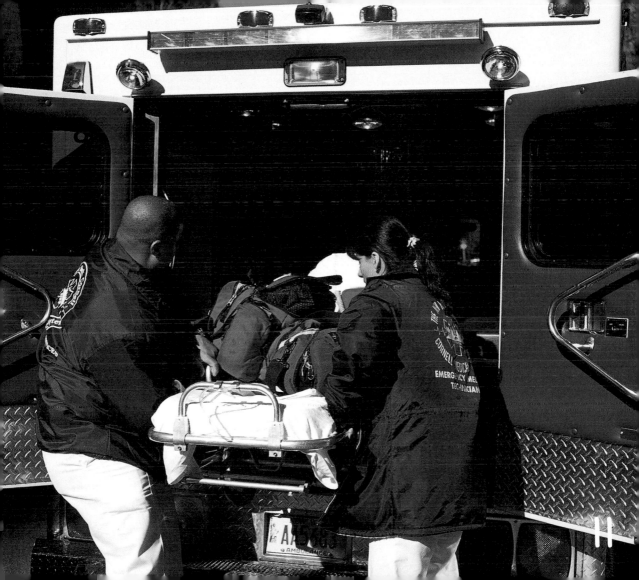

There's a woman who is sick!

Beatrice puts a **mask** on the woman.

It helps the woman to breathe.

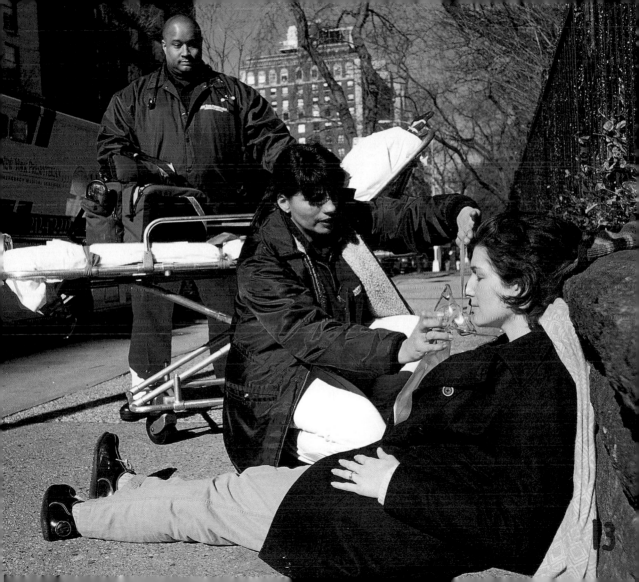

We put the woman in the ambulance.

We will take her to the hospital.

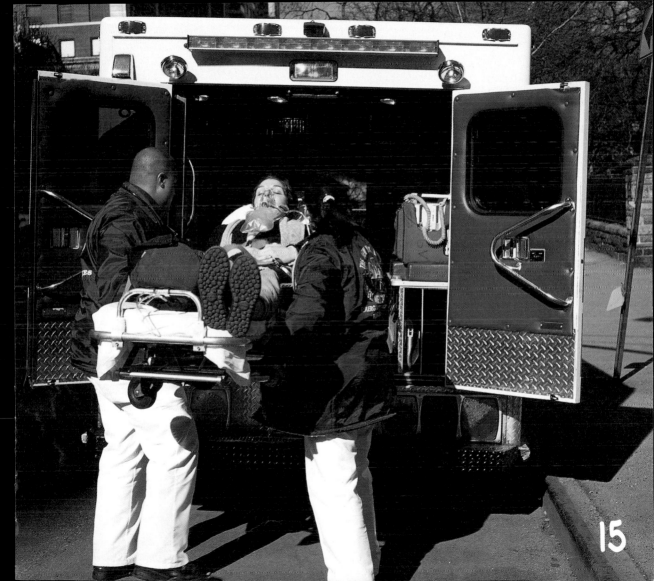

Beatrice stays in the back of the ambulance.

She **treats** the sick woman.

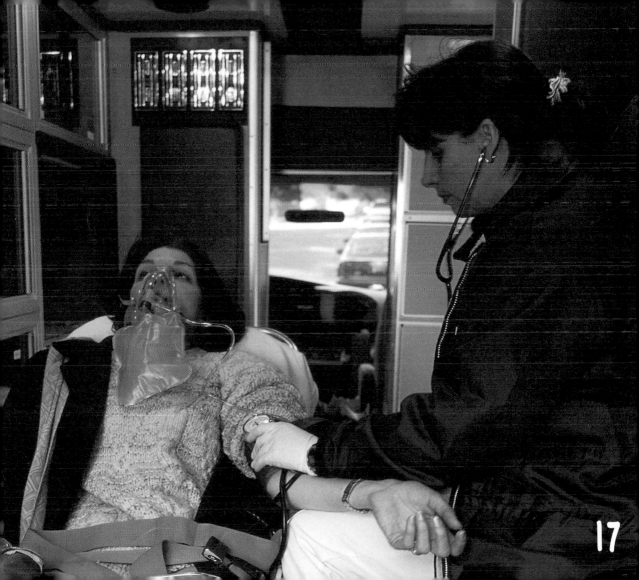

17

A doctor meets us at the hospital.

We tell the doctor what is wrong with the woman.

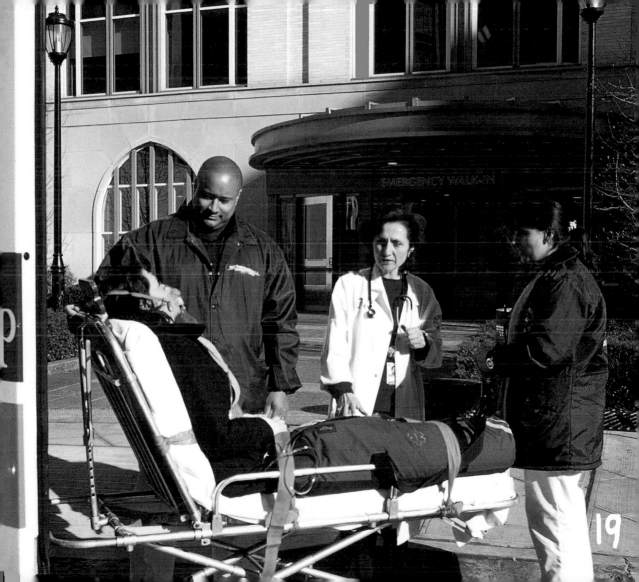

19

Our job is done.

Now we are ready for our next emergency.

New Words

ambulance (**am**-byu-lens) a truck that is used to take someone to the hospital

emergency (ee-**mir**-jen-see) a problem that needs attention right away

kit (**kit**) a bag of supplies used to treat someone

mask (**mask**) something that is put over a person's mouth and nose to help the person breathe

paramedics (par-e-**med**-ix) workers who treat people at an emergency

stretcher (**strech**-er) a cot with wheels to move someone who is hurt or sick

treats (**treetz**) cares for someone who is sick or hurt

22

To Find Out More

Books

Ambulances
by Marcia S. Freeman
Capstone Press

Emergency!
by Gail Gibbons
Holiday House

Impatient Pamela Calls 9-1-1
by Mary B. Koski
Trellis Publishing

Web Site
The Kid Zone
http://firefighting.com/emtsue/kids
Print out and color emergency pictures. There also is lifesaving information and tips for using 911.

Index

ambulance, 6, 10, 14, 16

doctor, 18

emergency, 8, 10, 20

hospital, 14, 18

kit, 10

mask, 12

paramedics, 4

radio, 6

stretcher, 10

treats, 16

About the Author
Jan Kottke is the owner/director of several preschools in the Tidewater area of Virginia. A lifelong early education professional, she is completing a phonics reading series for preschoolers.

Reading Consultants
Kris Flynn, Coordinator, Small School District Literacy, The San Diego County Office of Education

Shelly Forys, Certified Reading Recovery Specialist, W.J. Zahnow Elementary School, Waterloo, IL

Peggy McNamara, Professor, Bank Street College of Education, Reading and Literacy Program